DR PHIL CUMMINS
CHARACTER EDUCATION SERIES

Make a Difference

Make a
Difference

DR PHIL CUMMINS
CHARACTER EDUCATION SERIES

Make a
Difference

For the architects of my life.

Published in 2025 by Amba Press, Melbourne, Australia
www.ambapress.com.au

© Phil Cummins 2025

All rights reserved. No part of this book may be reproduced or transmitted in any form or by any means, electronic or mechanical, including photocopying, recording or by any information storage and retrieval system, without prior permission in writing from the publisher.

Cover design: Tess McCabe
Internal design: Amba Press
Editor: Rica Dearman

ISBN: 9781923215801 (pbk)
ISBN: 9781923215818 (ebk)

A catalogue record for this book is available from the National Library of Australia.

Contents

Foreword ix
Introduction: Make a Difference 1

Chapter 1
The things that matter — 5

Values and beliefs 9
Ethical decision-making 11
Self-regulation 14
Character 17
Step Forward and Up: The things that matter 22

Chapter 2
Telling your story — 23

Social purpose 28
Personal brand 30
Social recognition 32
Social impact 35
Step Forward and Up: Telling your story 39

Chapter 3
Getting it done   **41**

Goal setting   45
Planning   48
Project management   50
Evaluation   53
Step Forward and Up: Getting it done   57

Conclusion: Let's go!   59

Foreword

Hi! My name is Phil.

For more than thirty-five years, as an educator, researcher and speaker, I've been talking with and listening to hundreds of thousands of students, their families and teachers all over the world as they tell me what they want for their lives.

For as long as I can remember, I have been driven by a powerful need to make a difference in the world. As a younger man, I found this expressed through service to my family, the schools in which I taught and led, and in the contributions I made as a soldier. In more recent times, I have been inspired to connect with people all over the world through my enterprises, my writing, my podcast and my work with communities to find out what it is that we can do to achieve better outcomes for learners and their families. I don't know what form this sense of purpose might take into the future, but I know that I am not nearly finished yet.

What about you? What might be your narrative? What might be the reasons you seek to be a blessing for others? How might you grow in the character, competency and wellness you need to make a difference?

I think there are four ways you can grow in the character, competency and wellness throughout a life of being and becoming yourself:

1. **A Life of Purpose** – how to identify and claim the fundamental reason why for your journey of exploration, discovery and encounter.
2. **The Pathway to Excellence** – how to learn, live, lead and work as you strive to become the best version of yourself.
3. **Leading for Tomorrow's World** – how to connect your purpose to leadership which influences, inspires, directs and motivates others to build a shared vision for the future.
4. **Make a Difference** – how to create a plan to put your sense of purpose into practice for the sake of people and place and planet.

Drawing on the global research of three organisations that I lead (CIRCLE Education, a School for tomorrow. and the *Game Changers* podcast), I've written four books that explore in turn each of these four ways to grow in character. They're all about helping you to be well and grow in the knowledge, skills, dispositions and habits you need to understand what your purpose is and how you might learn, live, lead and work in pursuit of it.

This book, *Make a Difference*, is about finding a powerful and compelling narrative for your life, one that takes you from identifying and claiming your 'why?' to charting a way forward for the journey ahead.

So, what inspires you to be and do your best? What might you contribute? What will be your legacy? Are you ready to take the big Step Forward and Up to **Make a Difference**?

Let's go!

Phil

Dr Phil Cummins FRSA FACEL FIML
Managing Partner, a School for tomorrow.
Managing Director, CIRCLE – The Centre for Innovation,
   Research, Creativity and Leadership in Education
Associate Professor of Education and Enterprise
Honorary Senior Fellow, University of Melbourne
Host, *Game Changers* podcast

Introduction
Make a Difference

Can you tell me a story? Can you tell me your story? Can you tell me *our* story?

Storytelling is an inextricable part of the history and nature of our humanity. We've been telling stories for thousands of years. Nobody needs to tell us what a good story is – we know it when we hear it. We know it when we feel it, whether this is passed down to us through our DNA, our culture, our upbringing or all of the above.

Human beings need to feel as though there is both a purpose and a storyline in their lives. They feel rudderless unless they know that there is meaning to what happens and what they learn from these things that occur in their lives every day. For some, what is most meaningful might be family, for others, it's friends, and others again, it's career or cause. For many, it's a faith in the divine or the proper working of the planetary ecosystem or both. For most, it's a combination of all of these things in different degrees of importance.

For all, there's a meaning behind what they do. There's something that they're doing it for, a conclusion they're working towards. This, over time or immediately, might be embraced as a purpose. This is the fundamental reason for what it is that they do, the answer to their question of 'why am I doing this?'

Your sense of purpose needs to go further than this. It needs to make the effort of everyday life and the extra energy required to tackle significant challenges that appear in a myriad of other related questions that you might ask yourself: why am I going to work every day? Why am I studying? Why am I striving to be a better person? Who or what is this all for? That's where purpose really matters the most.

Your purpose changes over time, as what is most important and what seems to be the most worthwhile way to commit and use your personal and material resources adapts to the changes in your life. Your purpose will also reflect the ongoing wrestling between your inner drive and the requirements of your external circumstances.

The research of a School for tomorrow. (my global network dedicated to finding better outcomes for more learners) tells us that leaders around the world who genuinely care for people and place and planet align their inner and outer purpose in this way. They believe personally and professionally in the imperative to develop the character of their organisation so that they might thrive in their world.

Yet for many of these servant leaders, the busyness of life and their commitment to put the needs of others before themselves means they usually lack the reflective space to build a model for the character of their own purpose and how they put it into practice through their leadership. They rarely set goals to develop their own competencies in this respect. Their leadership often fails to improve because they can't link it to a theory that explains the decisions that drive them and the development of their organisations and communities.

I believe that all leaders can benefit from giving themselves an opportunity to sketch out what their model of practice looks like and how it connects to the ethos, strategy and operations of their organisation or community. In particular, from what we have seen, I'd argue that the quality and consistency of what occurs in their organisations largely results from the will and capacity of leaders to embed a shared commitment to 'what we want, why we want it and how we do it' in building the character, competency and wellness of all learners. In other words, the character of leaders shapes the character of the organisation.

As you travel this journey to build your character and to build the character of your team, organisation or community informed by a sense of purpose – in other words, to **Make a Difference** – you will also find that not all of this purpose is necessarily clear to you. It may take some time before you can articulate your purpose explicitly, in the same way that right now you might not be able to map all of the episodes of your life into one storyline. That's OK, but please be aware that while leadership through the implicit example you set is essential, you will be far more effective as a leader when you can explain to others (and yourself) what you are doing and why you are doing it.

You need a model to explain your 'way' to others and to yourself. With a model that explains the theory of your character and your leadership, and a story that explains how you put purpose into practice for the sake of people and place and planet and what you learned along the way, you can both convince others that what is needed can be done and that it is worth doing.

To **Make a Difference**, therefore, you need to be honest about your story and the story of your organisation. Hype, rhetoric and puff characterise too much of the current public discourse. I worry that too frequently we allow the line between aspiration and reality to become blurred to suit the purposes of those who want to convince us that down is up or up is down, for reasons which are not connected to a greater good framed within the sort of values that inform what it takes to thrive in our world.

Throughout this book, I will be asking you to reflect on your true self and what it might mean to **Make a Difference** that brings values and value to the lives of others. I'll also share with you some of my own story and what I have learned from it about how to become the best version of myself.

Are you ready to take your first step to **Make a Difference**?

Let's go!

Chapter 1
The things that matter

The things that matter

When I was a young man, I was challenged to name the things I stood for. I was questioned about my willingness to judge others for their values and character when I didn't know clearly what it was that I stood for myself.

It took me more than a little time to think about what I could say in answer to this question. Eventually, after about a week, I settled on three key ideas: loyalty, service and integrity. I asked the person if I could meet with them again and explain myself.

I am very grateful to this day for having gone through this experience. It taught me much about what it means to lead with values first and to allow a sense of purpose to emerge from those values.

I believe that you need to know what is important to you. By setting aside time and developing habits that work towards putting your values in action, you can build your understanding of what needs to happen next and how this might be done in a manner that reflects what you believe is good and right. You also need to know yourself, your strengths, and believe in your ability to improve. You can always be better at what you do.

To make progress in building your understanding of the things that matter and the character through which you will express this, you don't have to be perfect or extraordinary to succeed. You must simply aim for excellence and pursue it through a process of wrestling with your character, growing in your competency and building the wellness you need to become the best version of yourself

Chapter 1 is all about clarifying what is meaningful and important in your life. We will explore four key areas to help you discover what really matters:

1. Values and beliefs
2. Ethical decision-making
3. Self-regulation
4. Character

I'd like you to work through each in turn with me before you Step Forward and Up and begin to form a plan to **Make a Difference**.

Values and beliefs

Do you know what you stand for? Do you know the best way to put your values into action? How well do you make choices about what you will and will not do in your life based on your values?

We need to understand our place and responsibilities within the world. This is a lifelong challenge – the challenge of identity. On our journey towards this we will face many difficult decisions, life-changing moments and, of course, all the living that takes place in between. To navigate this, we need a system to understand what we do, why we do it and why it is important to us. The answers come from our core beliefs and moral code – the framework of values we use to make decisions and live our lives.

This is most important when life challenges us. As young people, we're expected to be able to do a lot: be a full-time student, engage in co-curricular activities, exercise, play a musical instrument, have lots of hobbies, a healthy social life and be responsible for the maintenance of our own lives. In moments where we are inundated with the day-to-day and feel like we cannot balance all of our tasks and responsibilities, the easy way out is to compromise on who we are as a person, take shortcuts or make uncharacteristic decisions – in order to make our lives easier. It is in moments like these that we need to be able to clear our mind and return to our core beliefs and moral code to recenter, refocus and recalibrate ourselves, in order to be the best that we can be.

The inspiration for our core beliefs and moral code comes from everything around us. We must nurture them and allow them to grow as we do. Looking to the world around us for opportunities to develop our understanding of our own humanity through others is a fundamental element of being a good person. Reading about, reflecting on and discussing with others our core beliefs and moral code provides us with opportunities to understand them better and, more importantly, to challenge them. This lifelong interrogation of our core beliefs and moral code is essential if we wish to grow as people and can be supported by looking outward as well as inward.

Finally, we need to consider the impact that our core beliefs and moral code will have on other people. Viewing our core beliefs and moral code as frameworks to support us in being better people, or in helping other people, is far more important than viewing them as mechanisms to drive material success. While goals and aspirations are important for our development and progress, our core beliefs and moral code are the driving force behind the type of person we are. When all is said and done, will the people around us remember us as a good person?

Your weaknesses are your weaknesses. They exist and you should not punish yourself about them. Over time, you should try to adopt new approaches and techniques to turn weaknesses into strengths and employ them to generate benefit for both you and others. At a School for tomorrow. we have learnt most of your solutions and successes will come from your strengths when they align with the values at the core of your being.

The process begins with an inward investigation and flows into an outward interrogation of the world around you. Therefore, the best starting point is identifying your own best character strengths – the knowledge, skills, dispositions and habits that equip, empower and enable you for growth, progress and success. You will need to build a framework to align your values with your actions through your strengths.

Your values are only useful to the extent you commit to applying them in your life. This requires you to learn to believe in yourself, your strengths and how to stand by them. It is important to feel confident in yourself in a non-judgemental setting; you need to have a healthy relationship with your external world – the people around you and the expectations they set for you and others in your life – to embark on this process of growth.

> ### REFLECTION: VALUES AND BELIEFS
>
> Please consider the following questions:
>
> Do I have a set of beliefs that serve me well as an anchor for everything I do?
>
> Even when things get tough, would I unknowingly or willingly violate or compromise my core beliefs?
>
> Am I always seeking to explore and deepen my core beliefs through reading, reflection and discussion with others?
>
> Is it important for me to live with purpose and integrity?
>
> Does acting on my core beliefs and moral code improve the lives of others and are they a source of good, not just personal gain?

Ethical decision-making

Can you make choices in your life based on what you think is right? How consistently do you do this? Can you identify the correct options to live a good life based on your core beliefs and moral code?

The choices we make in our day-to-day lives grow to define us as people. Once we have identified our core beliefs and moral code, we should next consider how these apply to our lives. Ethical decision-making is about adopting an approach to forming choices based on our values. This approach will help us to identify the good and right answers so that we can live a life based on the appreciation of what is good and right, according to our core beliefs and moral code.

Every day, we face many opportunities and challenges. Though all differ in size, importance and complexity, each requires decisions to be made. In every moment, we have the power and autonomy to be true to ourselves, and act in a way that reflects who we are at this moment, as well as the person we want to become. It is important that these decisions align with our core beliefs and moral code. If not, we are likely to feel guilt, regret and disappointment in both ourselves and the world we have created by acting unethically.

Some decisions require more attention than others. Important ethical dilemmas that keep us up at night require investigation. This often means an effort to identify all possible solutions and consider which course of action aligns best with our own morality. Seeking counsel from our family, friends and the people we look up to or applying ethical frameworks can be very useful in this process. But in both cases, we must have a clear understanding of our own ethics and morality first and foremost. These need to be the markers we return to in order to judge how we have acted.

We often find ourselves in situations where it is incredibly difficult to make the right decision. Sometimes this might be because others pressure us, or it might be because we feel pressure to live up to an expectation we have set for ourselves. But it is normal to want to do something for an immediate reward; it is difficult to understand the importance of the big picture. To overcome these expectations, we need to build a sense of moral resilience – a sense of validation in being a good person. This doesn't mean we are negative about or look down on others; it means we set a high standard and hold ourselves accountable when we don't meet it.

The reason why we act ethically is also important. We should act ethically because there is value in being a good person. The world becomes a better, kinder place when we all worry a little less about ourselves and care a little more about others. Doing the right thing should not be underwritten by a desire for congratulations or credit; come solely with the hope of receiving something commensurate in return; or simply look forward to a future payoff.

No one will get it right one hundred per cent of the time; we will get it wrong a lot of the time, and that's OK. As we grow older and commit to the process of ethical decision-making, our margin of error will fluctuate. Over time, we will feel more comfortable making difficult decisions that put the needs of others first. Slowly and surely, we will stop doing things because we see something in it for ourselves, and we will start doing them because they are the right thing to do.

Reflection: Ethical decision-making

Please consider the following questions:

Do I have a clear sense of what is the 'right thing' to do, and can I confidently apply this to the daily and sometimes difficult decisions I make?

Do I have a full understanding of what I need to do to meet all ethical standards for academic honesty and integrity in my studies?

Am I confident that I would choose to do the right thing even if doing so had negative consequences?

Have I made mistakes in the past in my ethical judgement but learnt from these to make me better?

Do I let pressure or circumstance override my sense of what's right and what's wrong?

Self-regulation

Do you know how you learn? Can you recognise your emotions and respond constructively to them? Are you developing the self-awareness and self-mastery needed to postpone the need for instant pleasure in the pursuit of a longer-term objective?

Self-regulation means taking responsibility for and following through with how you organise yourself and your life in accordance with your values and aspirations. When you feel that you have a plan in place and the tools to do the things you need to do, you will need execution and commitment to complete the task, achieve the goal or enact the change that you believe is important. Self-regulation, therefore, is the ability to do what you say you will do and stick to it.

As you learn, live, lead and work on your journey of exploration, discovery and encounter, you will need to think about how you will respond to your inner drive and the expectations of those around you. Your contribution will be measured in terms of the high standards that you uphold. You will need to stay true to your values and those of your community while also improving the lives of others and getting the job done.

Ensuring that values are upheld while value is created in your planning and project management starts with your self-belief. You need to have confidence in how you organise yourself to get the job done and in your capacity to move with change to achieve what you set out to do before you get started. You will need to look at your past performance, your willingness to put your purpose into practice and the character, competencies and wellness you have that underpin this.

Your self-regulation will also need to set an example for those around you. Your ability to achieve things in the right way and with respect for people and place and planet will help those around you to be the same. They will also see the methods that are most likely to work to this end. You should, therefore, communicate widely about your belief that 'we' can do it while we reflect on how we are going to do it.

Self-regulation relies on your ability to manage your time and yourself. Whether your parameters are set by you or by someone or something else, all of your goals, projects and tasks have due dates. You need to plan and work within these boundaries and identify what needs to be done, in what order, and what information and resources you will need. You need to allocate time to each piece of work. This will allow you to define your scope and sequence.

And then you need to get stuck into the work and get it done!

Building a track record of commitment to the goal and execution of the plan will help you to develop the sense of mastery, autonomy and purpose you need to remain motivated. You then need to track and evaluate your progress, record the achievement of your milestones and reward yourself along the way. If you play to your strengths, you can build your capacity to adhere to the task at hand. This process will require you to make temporary sacrifices for long-term reward.

This is where self-control and judgement come into play. You need to recognise when you are doing good work and when you are not. You need to hold yourself accountable to the process you have designed. You need to understand which of your behaviours are helping you to move forward, and do more of them. Likewise, you need to identify which behaviours are holding you back and try to cut them out. You also need to be able to regulate your emotions so that you can promote positive behaviours and delay the impulse to act on less productive behaviours.

Utilising your resources is also important. You should bring in other people to support you with your plan. If you share your process and goals, you can create a means for supervision and external accountability that can help you to build good habits. Good habits will then help you to shape your internal motivation – this will be the most powerful driver of your self-regulation in the long run. The more disciplined you are, the better you will feel about yourself, and the more likely you will be to keep running towards the prize.

> ### Reflection: Self-regulation
>
> Please consider the following questions:
>
> Do I have the resilience to overcome setbacks and to frame mistakes as opportunities to learn?
>
> Am I developing my sense of self-efficacy as I develop my goals, pursue my ambitions, and learn how to adapt to change and uncertainty?
>
> Do I have good time-management and work habits, and do I continue to refine and improve these to meet new expectations, standards and challenges?
>
> Am I prepared to make sacrifices today in order to gain success and achieve my career goals?
>
> Do I control my reactions to difficulties, tensions and disagreements with others and find ways to strengthen productive collaboration?

Character

Do you belong? Are you realising your potential? Are you doing what is good and right?

Character is the way we live life. It's how we wrestle with what's inside us and what's expected of us. It comprises the civic character of belonging, the performance character of achieving potential, and the moral character of doing good and right in the world.

The journey of learning towards character needs to connect us to the essential questions that we all have and point us towards a way to find answers to them. The power of this inquiry to help us all to live better lives, feel as though we are making a difference and know we are getting somewhere, must be sourced in the message we use to talk about it. It must be so significant, so rich and perhaps even so disruptive of our frames of mind that it compels us to sit up and take notice. It must force us to want to do something about it. It must make us commit to finding our way and taking a big step forward and up.

To ask and answer important questions like the ones at the beginning of this section, you must dig deep within yourself to find an inner sense of where you are in the story of who you have been, who you are and who you might become. This is called your personal 'mark'. You must also identify your 'measure', or how you are trying to live up to others' expectations. Developing your character is about wrestling with both your mark and your measure. As you wrestle with yourself and your context, you will grow in the civic character of belonging, the performance character of realising your potential, and the moral character of doing what is good and right.

Character is never constant, nor is it ever fully formed. It is a perfect exemplar of both the potential we have to make a difference and also of the fragility of our human existence.

None of us, therefore, can ever be whole in our character; there will always be cracks that may even go deep into the core of who we are, what we do and why we do it in search of belonging, the fulfilment of potential, and the attempt to do good and right in the world. This is why we are meant to live in community; this is why we need to rely on our interdependence with each other. We need to build others up so that, together, we might be stronger and better.

When we lead others, one thing we do is to transform singular journeys towards character into the ongoing quest for a family, team, company or nation as to how we should live a life together. When cracks appear, we let the light shine in through our story so that we might go forward together.

In other words, our individual character becomes our collective character and is reflected in how we learn, live, lead and work together. If we can bring together a group of people and influence, inspire, direct and motivate them to get the job done, and to help us all know ourselves, earn our places, go on a journey and find our calling, and if we can help them to do this together, then we will know that we have led them well.

Do you see how this works? The character of our leadership shapes the character of those whom we lead. In particular, the growth in character, competency and wellness that we as individuals, organisations and communities need to thrive is propelled through relationships specifically designed for this type of learning, which is called character apprenticeship.

Character apprenticeship relationships occur when learners are accepted as novices by experts who coach, model and scaffold for them how to learn, live, lead and work. Novices explore, articulate and reflect on this, craft their self-efficacy and acquire adaptive expertise in their own right.

Adaptive expertise means how human beings grow in our character competencies and wellness, and then how we use these things to solve known and new problems. It is, in essence, our commitment to growth. And then there's self-efficacy, which means how we organise ourselves and our learning, living, leadership and work to optimise our character competencies and wellness so that they can thrive in our world. Self-efficacy is our capacity to be the best versions of ourselves.

Learning and growth are typically proven through times of trial when matters test and stretch resilience and robustness. Experts yield the power they held at first as voice, agency and advocacy are demonstrated; they take on the role of wise counsellors as their once-novices leave the close proximity of the apprenticeship. In turn and in time, the former novices-turned-experts pass on to their own novices the knowledge, skills, dispositions and habits that comprise their competency, and the character and wellness on which their adaptive expertise and self-efficacy is grounded. The cycle continues and through the character of individuals, organisations and communities are formed and strengthened.

How we do this work of character apprenticeship daily in no small measure determines the success of what we do. We take on those with whom we come into contact through work, education or community and we agree to support their growth. We do this to help them to find that inner sense of who they need to become and articulate that through their evolving perspective of the world.

Great leadership takes us on a journey to become the best version of ourselves. To do this, we need to feel as though we belong, fulfil our potential, and do good and right in the world. We need to be able to relate to people and they need to be able to relate to us.

If we can relate through the experience of belonging, the fulfilment of potential, and the doing of what is good and right, we can connect. If we can connect through how we learn, live, lead and work, then together we can achieve. To comprehend our achievement and the pathway towards it, we need a vision of where we're going and how we might get there.

We need to tell a story of yesterday, today and tomorrow, one in which each of us can see how we play a part that enhances our individual and collective sense of dignity and worth. That's the character that will help you to **Make a Difference**.

> ### Reflection: Character
>
> Please consider the following questions:
>
> Can I identify my best character strengths – those character skills and habits that contribute most to my success and wellbeing and that I rely on most often and effectively?
>
> Do I often see character strengths in others that I admire and wish I could have, too? Is it important for me to live with purpose and integrity?
>
> Do I take the view that, with focus and effort, I can work on my character strengths and develop new ones, rather than seeing them as fixed and immutable?
>
> Is it important to me that my character strengths contribute to the success and wellbeing of others, and not just myself?
>
> Am I becoming competent in reflecting on and setting goals to align my values and character through my competencies?

Step Forward and Up

The things that matter

The development and mastery of putting your values in action is a lifelong process. I've written throughout the **Character Education Series** about the values I have learned from my research and personal experience that I have adopted to help guide my life:

- ✓ Meaningfulness – for good
- ✓ Authenticity – for real
- ✓ Transformation – for change
- ✓ Sustainability – for life
- ✓ Selflessness – for others
- ✓ Relationality – for each other

What is your list? What are the things that matter to you?

Write a short statement that describes your values and beliefs – your moral code.

When you are ready, let's move on to Chapter 2 to think about how you might align these values and beliefs to develop a sense of purpose that tells your story.

Let's go!

Chapter 2
Telling your story

Telling your story

I shared with you earlier in the **Character Education Series** some of my story:

> I'm a son of immigrant families. I was born and educated on Gadigal land in Sydney; I now live on Wurundjeri Woiwurrung country in the greatest suburb in the world – Fitzroy, Melbourne.
>
> I began teaching History and Latin many years ago. Since then, I've worked in and with schools, travelling the world as a leader, colleague and professor of education and enterprise. I've done quite a few other things as well. I've been a father to three children; I've worked for my local church and its community; I've served my country as a soldier. I've written a lot of books and articles – millions of words in history and education, particularly about the strategy, leadership, governance and culture that help to describe an authentic vision for learning and make real its power to transform the lives of students, their families and teachers.

I love telling a story and finding the structure behind the narrative. I love working out where the voice, agency and advocacy lie in human affairs (as well as those that lie beyond) and, of course,

I love thinking about the reasons why. I'm an optimist, so I believe that stories should end well. I believe that a positive attitude, seeing the best in others, a willingness to work hard and the wit to adapt what's at hand to deal with what life throws up are essential.

Young people all over the world tell me that they want to connect with something that goes beyond their own emotional, intellectual and physical selves. They want to embark on a journey of exploration and discovery in which they encounter self-awareness, relationship, service and vocation that takes them beyond self-interest towards selflessness. The key assumption that underpins this is that a life of giving to others is transformative for each of us because it is grounded in the genuine meaningfulness that equips, empowers and enables us for a life of purpose.

I know what this means for me. I've decided that I'm going to spend the rest of my career working towards helping people to feel as though they belong, can fulfil their potential, and do good and right things because they have been educated through the transforming power of a future-fit education for character, competency and wellness. I want to help them to find and claim their purpose, to become the best versions of themselves by putting this purpose into practice for the sake of people and place and planet throughout their lives. This is my vocation, my calling, the purpose for which I am being formed and towards which I am directing my career.

What about you? What is your story?

All of us need to learn how to tell a story about ourselves and how we contribute to the world around us. None of us is perfect, so neither should our stories be perfect. No amount of superficial curation of a public image via social media or other means can make up for a lack of substance as a person or an inability to take responsibility and do things of lasting quality and benefit. For a while, you can fool yourself and maybe others as well, but in the end, your personal brand will be exposed if there is a gap between what you say and what you do. People need to be able to trust you and rely on you.

If you stand up for what is right, do what you say you will do and seek not to harm others or place your interests before the greater good, you can generate a strong and positive story over time by building a reputation as a person whose purpose and presence align to create a positive social impact on the world around you.

Chapter 2 is all about *your* story. We will explore four key areas to help you bring meaning and shape to this:

1. Social purpose
2. Personal brand
3. Social recognition
4. Social impact

I'd like you to work through each in turn with me before you Step Forward and Up and continue your plan to **Make a Difference**.

Social purpose

Who are the people most important to you? Where are the places that are important to you? What is your sense of connection to our planet? How would you like to contribute to all of them?

Each of us needs a purpose in life that is higher than ourselves. It is natural for us to be self-centred, to believe that what directly affects us is the most important thing in the world. Yet, there is nothing more powerful in the world to move us individually and collectively than selflessness – you will find that putting others before yourself will be the secret to your success.

This quest to achieve a social purpose does not mean you should allow yourself and your good intentions to be exploited by others. Nor does it mean you should neglect your own wellness for the sake of others – you can't be much use to others if you don't look after yourself! As you find a social purpose that feels right to you, you will find that this can motivate you beyond self-interest. You will be working towards and achieving that fundamentally important thing that sits well with your values and that also brings value to you and those around you.

To build values and create value, you will need to work out what is important to you and your community. Think about this in terms of the values (ideas and beliefs about what is good and right) and value (necessary and desirable things that you can give and receive that will improve the lives of others). Both of these can tell you much about how you might share opportunities, resources, accomplishments and hardships as you create community together.

What is most important is how you can direct your own character and competency to help others. You will find that this can become the driving force behind how you develop and apply the civic character of belonging, the performance character of achieving your potential, and the moral character of doing what is good and right towards something that the world really needs. In this way, you can connect 'my purpose' to 'my people' and 'my place'. You should also think about the impact this will have on 'my planet' so that you gain an even wider understanding of what really motivates you beyond yourself.

As you move forward with your social purpose, be willing to take risks. Stick with your mission until you are successful or until it is no longer of value. Remember that the sudden appearance of a roadblock will leave you with no choice but to create a Plan B. When things get tough and you are making a decision, remember to pause, regroup and try again.

Your commitment to your journey to make a difference, inspired by your social purpose, can become the most significant reason for who you are and who you might become. Armed with a purpose for your humanity, values and value for your community, and an inside-out process of growth, you can give yourself the best chance of an exciting adventure and a happy future for you and all those around you.

Reflection: Social purpose

Please consider the following questions:

Can I explain my purpose and show how it is aligned with the mission of the organisation in which I work and lead?

Does my purpose respond to the place where I work and lead – the culture, ethos, relationships and ways by which results are achieved?

> Is my purpose in service of the progress and wellness of the people with whom I work and lead?
>
> Does my purpose guide my practice – how I act, manage and lead to meet my responsibilities and to ensure that the organisation achieves its goals and results?
>
> How might I refine, deepen and strengthen my purpose over the course of my journey?

Personal brand

Who are you? How do you reveal your identity to others? What does this say about your story?

A brand originally referred to the way a branding iron left a mark on cattle, signifying ownership. In our world today, a personal brand refers to both the mark and measure of a person – how you express what is at the core of who you are and how you aim up to the expectations of others. It also refers to the reputation you earn that is connected to your story.

Each of us tells a story of our lives. This story is partly a narrative of yesterday, today and tomorrow. It allows you to project to others the best version of yourself – what you stand for and against, what you believe is important, and how you go about trying to set and achieve your goals.

What you should strive for is an authentic brand – how others see you needs to reflect what is real, true and good about you. You will, therefore, need to adopt an ethical approach towards your personal branding – how you can build a reputation for doing what is good and right according to your core beliefs and moral code. A key part of this will be your honesty and taking responsibility for your mistakes.

A personal brand of true influence and repute is created when individuals act with conviction and character: they bring values and value to the lives of others. Your brand story will live in the minds of others, particularly because of how you demonstrate your strength of character and how it improves the lives of others. How do you use kindness, consideration and respect to help others to feel as though they belong? How do you show the resilience, professionalism and decision-making ability that underscores your performance? How do your honesty, selflessness and service demonstrate your moral code?

You can help make the world a better, kinder and more productive place by living with love, integrity and genuine care for others. It will connect with what people expect of you and gradually becomes the cornerstone of your reputation.

Your reputation for good character will become part of your personal brand over time. It is how you appear in the minds and hearts of others. It will take ongoing and conscious effort for you to build a personal brand that will make you and those you care for proud of who you are and who you are becoming.

Your personal brand will also require you to be professional. You must be genuine in your desire to achieve success as a team and as an individual, and for others to know this. Setting high standards for your own work and holding others to high standards shows how much you value performance. It's also important to strive for excellence while maintaining modesty and good manners. Others will be more inclined to believe in who you are as you establish a personal brand that says you are a quality person who generates high-quality work and that you encourage, support and inspire others to be and do the same.

> **Reflection: Personal Brand**
>
> Please consider the following questions:
>
> Do I uphold honesty and good values in my personal and professional life?
>
> Do I set high standards for my work?
>
> Am I a good decision-maker who uses information wisely, consults effectively and thinks creatively?
>
> Do I communicate clearly and effectively, and can I convey difficult concerns and solutions?
>
> Am I a servant leader who builds community?

Social recognition

How do others see you? What does this say about you? What purpose does your public self bring to your community?

Throughout your journey to **Make a Difference**, you need to work out how to earn proper social recognition – how to make choices and be acknowledged for those you make for yourself and others in your community. Social recognition helps us to believe that the things we are doing are important, that the people around us accept and love us for who we are, and that we have value.

Your actions should not be contrived to get praise or flattery, but rather to be genuine and authentic. You need to do what you say you will do, not just say whatever it takes to impress others. Genuineness and perseverance are valued more than over-promising and under-delivering. Accepting this and committing to quality will grow your reputation because you will be aligning your values with the value that others see in you.

You are more likely to gain appropriate social recognition if you can show that who you are, what you are doing and who you are becoming is laid on a foundation of strong and positive character. The quality and consistency of your performance, therefore, will earn you social recognition. Are you a person who strives for excellence in whatever you do? Do you value quality in your work, relationships and goals? Do you hold yourself to this standard and pause to reflect and refine your approach when you fall short?

Your reputation will be influenced especially by the way you are interested in and prioritise the success and wellness of others.

Each of us has a different need to be in the public eye. Do you want your voice to be heard? Do you want your actions to be acknowledged for their quality? Do you want your contributions to be valued? Your social standing and how others perceive you will influence how you feel about yourself. You will also need to connect your sense of purpose to how you care for people and place and planet that will enable you to earn your place in your communities as a person of character and excellence.

How do you see yourself in the public eye?

You are a complex and unique person with purpose, values and something of value to offer others. Like all of us, you need to pursue a personal journey of exploration to discover meaningfulness and encounter what is true and relevant.

As you learn more about your purpose and how this might be fulfilled through self-awareness, relationship, selflessness and vocation, you will need to learn to accept who you are today and strive to become the person you should become tomorrow. No doubt you can recognise the character and competencies of others and appreciate the things that they offer as a result. If you can do this forothers, then you should also learn to do this for yourself.

How will you be remembered? Your legacy will be the sum of your social recognition: who you were, who you became, how you responded to your mistakes and difficulties, and how you helped others. The process of building social recognition begins with how you engage with the process of honestly and unashamedly becoming a better version of yourself by doing this in community with others. It's about thriving in a way that is both personally fulfilling and also dedicated to the service of others, especially where it helps them to transform themselves and the community in which they live. Ultimately, your social recognition should reflect your character and the substance of your willingness to create a life of purpose.

Reflection: Social Recognition

Please consider the following questions:

Are my ethics and principles respected?

Do others think my purpose and how I put it into practice is worthwhile, accomplished and impactful?

Are the achievements and reputation of the team, group or organisation essential to me?

> Do I want to be remembered as someone who demonstrated respectful interpersonal relationships?
>
> Do I want to be recognised for my high-quality work and contribution?

Social impact

What impact do you want to have? What values and value do you bring to your world to achieve this aim? What is the difference that you want to make for others?

Your social impact is about how you bring values and value to others by setting and achieving goals that fulfil your social purpose. Your impact, therefore, arises from your belief in the importance of helping others, understanding what you can do about this and how the two intersect.

It is in this process of connecting 'your purpose' to 'your practice' in service of 'your people' and 'your place' that you may find a compelling reason that calls you to action – your sense of vocation. If you recognise and accept a call to fulfil a specific purpose for the benefit of others, you also need to accept that this will carry with it a set of responsibilities.

Understanding how you can use your character and competencies to create the right social impact is the first step towards fulfilling your responsibilities. The things you have learned through your life experience, education and relationships that make you who you are can all be used to help others understand their path.

Your knowledge, skills, dispositions and habits can all contribute towards achieving your social impact.

It's important to be conscious of the possibility for you to bring about tangible changes for the better of others. This awareness of your potential for social impact will be a great motivator for you. You need to feel as though you can make a difference, even if it's on a very small scale. Your determination – that what we do will result in better outcomes for at least one other person – really matters for you and for others.

Your willingness to serve by putting others' interests first will also provide a role model for others. These qualities and your demonstration of them will attract other like-minded people to your cause – those who share and can contribute to your values. Together, you can build a genuine community of inquiry and practice. When we have others around us, we can do more through the relationships we build than we can by ourselves. It does become more complicated, but it should be more rewarding and fun for you.

So, how then might you begin to dedicate yourself to creating your desired social impact? You are more likely to generate positive goodwill and tangible outcomes for others in your immediate and existing connections: your family and friends. How might you spend time improving their lives either by removing a burden that you might be placing upon them or by relieving them of another burden? Do you do your fair share of chores at home? Do you spend as much time, if not more time, working on your friends' problems as they spend working on your own? Are there projects that your friends and family are committed to that you could give more of your time to? Could you learn competencies of leadership that would help you to take on further responsibilities in your immediate network?

Your social impact, of course, should not end here. You can and should, in due course, extend the boundaries of your influence and the extent of your impact. You can start to have a wider and more global impact if you take on the responsibility to contribute across more areas that impact upon more people. There is no shortage of opportunities to do things that will have a positive social impact on the world.

What is it that you can do now that might be of the greatest help to those that need it?

Be prepared to start from the ground up with many hours of quiet, unglamorous and dedicated service to others. If you want to change the world, start locally. You have a lot to learn from community service like mowing lawns, reading to children, supporting clean-up initiatives and volunteering your time with the elderly.

Above all, remember that creating a desired social impact means achieving the results that will bring this about. Your intentions, vision and action are important, as are your sociability and connectedness to others. You need to put your purpose into practice – to make this happen, together with your community, you will need to use a combination of humility and willpower that can make the promise of what once seemed impossible (or even improbable) actually happen.

> ### Reflection: Social Impact
>
> Please consider the following questions:
>
> Do I put my talents, knowledge and skills at the service of others?
>
> What benefits do I bring to those with whom I work and also the wider community?

Does how I lead and work help more people to feel as though they belong in my organisation and my community?

Does my personal sense of social purpose and social impact align with the mission of the organisations with which I am associated?

Does how I lead and work motivate others to tackle challenges by making sound decisions and designing innovative solutions?

Step Forward and Up
Telling your story

As we saw in Chapter 1, your values and beliefs tell you what is important in your world. These values and beliefs can become so important to you that they can come to define and underpin your rationale for living, your fundamental reason why you do what you do and make all of the choices that go along with this – **Purpose**. They connect you to and ground you in your relationships with others and the physical space you inhabit. The sense of belonging and responsibility emerges from these – **People and Place and Planet**. They bring the moral power of striving to do what is good and right to your attempts to fulfil your potential – **Practice**.

Your social purpose, therefore, is how you connect People and Place and Planet to your own sense of Purpose and put this into Practice. It is the fundamental reason you must bring both values and value to others. It starts with a sense inside you of what is right and wrong and then flows out into your actions and engagement with people and place and planet – your practice. It should be present in all of your relationships. It should grow and change as you do.

Think about the following questions:

- ✓ What difference do you want to make?
- ✓ What difference do you want to make in the lives of others?
- ✓ What contribution can you make in the years to come?
- ✓ What can you do right now?

Use the diagram on the previous page to sketch a map that you can use to tell your story. Define each term (People, Place, Planet, Purpose and Practice) in the statement in a way that makes sense to you. Use enough words to be specific, but not so many that you won't be able to remember it later.

When you write your statement of purpose, it doesn't have to be your 'forever purpose' or be too grand. You just need enough clarity to find the right direction for your energy, enthusiasm and capability now and into the next stage of your life. It might grow into something else over time, and that's OK. Identifying who, what and where you want to commit yourself to for now is a great starting point.

Take your time to think through what you have written and what you have learned so far. You have identified and are about to commit yourself to a social purpose that will require your effort, time and resources. Are you sure that this is right for you? Are you being realistic in your scope? Are there any refinements that you want to make to this?

When you are ready, let's start Chapter 3 so we can see how you can realise this remarkable statement of intention that you have for life.

Let's go!

Chapter 3
Getting it done

Getting it done

Are you the sort of person who gets things done? Are you the sort of person who is likely to put your purpose into practice? How will you need to improve your knowledge, skills, disposition and habits to help you do this? How can you infuse all of this with your love for others and how you put it into everything you do?

Through the example and encouragement of others in my life, I have built a lifelong habit of reflection on what it is that I do to get things done.

I think that a disposition towards driving forward is the best way to do what I do as a learner and a leader. As I build confidence and competency in what I am doing, I find that I can come to know in time that I am doing a good job. I recognise that I can't ever do this by standing still, by believing that I have already mastered everything or have already done it all, or that it's not possible for me to grow.

I am very deliberate about the need to keep going. If what I am doing doesn't work, I can either give it another go or learn from the experience and try something else to find another way forward. I prefer to incline to the things that work, but I also understand that

I have to allow myself the time either to grow in success or to exhaust the reasonable possibility of achieving something that warrants continued allocation and expenditure of resources.

I have to work hard not to take myself too seriously, especially when I make the sorts of mistakes that make me cross because I can't seem to escape them. As a result, there's often a practised playfulness, or an experimentation, about what I do that I use to counter my intensity.

The feeling of a meaningful calling to engage in the work of change for the better in the lives of others in your world is often called a vocation. Your sense of vocation guides relationship between your 'reason why' and how you serve those around you, by taking it from intention to reality, and can be a very powerful force in your life. It's how you can find your calling within the supportive network of people for and with whom your sense of belonging, the fulfilment of your potential and your propensity to do good and right can come together.

Chapter 3 is all about making your vocation come to life. We will explore four key areas to help you create a positive legacy for those around you:

1. Goal setting
2. Planning
3. Project management
4. Evaluation

Let's work through each in turn before you Step Forward and Up one last time and complete your plan to **Make a Difference**.

Goal setting

Do you know what you want to achieve? Do you understand the steps you need to take to make sure this happens? Do you set goals regularly?

Setting a goal means defining what you want to do and later whether or not you have achieved it. This should be followed up by a plan to identify what needs to happen to move this goal from intention to reality and, finally, result!

Your goals need to be specific, reasonable and achievable. Being practical and realistic doesn't mean you shouldn't aim high. It means you need to grasp the need for taking shorter legs on a longer journey – this is where short-term and long-term goals help you fit together the pieces of the journey. They help you to describe the process you need to take to grow in character, competency and wellness.

What is most important in goal setting is defining your intention: what you want to happen and what you need to do to achieve this. This is really important in giving you direction and helping you to feel good about who you are and who you are becoming. When this is happening, you will begin to see the value you are creating for yourself and for others in the person you are becoming and the growth and achievement that supports this.

If you are equipped with the knowledge that what you are proposing to do is both of value to you and others and is also in accordance with what you think is good and right, your goals will give you the sense of purpose you need to define your 'why?' and the courage to define the 'what?' that will lead in turn to the 'how?' that creates a roadmap for your journey.

The process of creating value through your goal setting begins with the decision to do the things that you want and need to do to become more fully *you*. Your goals also need to align with your values and beliefs about what matters most. If you don't know what's essential to you, then defining a goal that lacks this grounding in your sense of purpose is likely to leave you feeling let down, regardless of whether you succeed in accomplishing it. At the same time, if you apply your goals and success to an objective that is not linked to your sense of purpose in life, you risk achieving a hollow victory. The wins will more likely come when you bring value to the lives of others because you are growing in your own accomplishment capacity to achieve a purpose that is greater than you.

Often when you begin setting goals, you can lack experience in how to describe them; you can also lack confidence in how to apply them to an understanding of the bigger picture of our lives. You will paint this picture of your life much more successfully if you can assemble its elements correctly. For you to create a masterpiece, you need to see it as a blank canvas. Your long-term goals are comparable to a painting's major elements, while your short-term goals are like the brushstrokes that create those elements. All are necessary for a complete and meaningful product.

You will find that building an understanding of the sorts of things that you might want to do for your career will help you to take your goals and put them into a much more meaningful and purposeful context. When you set yourself clear objectives that have context in your life and are connected to your sense of purpose, you will have a good reason to wake up every day and to keep going when things become difficult.

Each of us responds well to achieving goals; they motivate us to aim higher and do more. Setting goals helps you enhance your abilities and performance, and increases what it means to realise your potential and the chances that you might do this. This is because goal setting changes how your brain is structured. As you move from the ambiguity of not knowing what you want to do to defining your aspirations and objectives, your brain becomes optimised to achieve those goals. The obstacles you perceive will reduce in size and the task will become much more doable.

Setting goals means being clear about a vision of your preferred future and how you will get there through how you learn, live, lead and work. The clarity that your goals in each of these competencies can give to the way you connect today with tomorrow will help to influence, inspire, direct and motivate you through the often tough effort required to get there.

Reflection: Goal setting

Please consider the following questions:

Are my thinking and planning grounded in my sense of purpose that informs the numerous choices that will comprise my career journey?

Do I know where and how to research sources that give me knowledge about and insight into the career areas that interest me?

Do I know how to find and connect to those who can help me evaluate and make good decisions about my career interests, pathway and goals?

Do I avoid rigid thinking in my career planning, knowing that I may need to adjust and adapt to changing circumstances and opportunities?

Do I know that I need to develop my character, competencies and wellness in order to thrive along my journey?

Planning

What is planning? How can you use plans to give substance to your aspirations? How can you be confident about creating your preferred future?

A plan isn't just a piece of paper with ideas about what you might do – it's an entire process that you engage with throughout your journey. Plans help you to devise new and better ways of doing things, assume greater responsibility, and make sound decisions for the benefit of others and yourself.

Plans consist of your intentions, your vision of what success will look like if these intentions are carried out, and the actions you will take to create success for you and your community. You take your goals and figure out your strategies, define tasks and work out what's required to make them happen. You revisit this plan continuously, refining your ideas and moving your goals forward as you make progress.

Your plans, therefore, are the living map for your entire journey. They evolve with you as you grow, develop, fail and achieve. The effectiveness of your planning will hinge on your ability to engage with your team and community through your planning and decision-making, and how you will build your own capacity to set and achieve goals.

In order to reach the objectives that you set, you need to plan ahead. Breaking things down into smaller, more manageable actions can help, although not every scenario can be pulled into separate parts. You may need to figure out how basic problems are related, or why there is no easy answer. You will need to realise that not everything can be done and that there is no perfect solution. This is normal, and developing an approach to managing this improves both your organisational skills and your ability to manage yourself.

Turning big ideas and hopes into fruition requires strong knowledge of who you are, where you are going and what you might encounter along the way. Your attention to detail will be crucial. Living in a community entails planning with and for others. It's a mission to connect with others that starts with questions: what is your moral code? How well do you value others? How well do you know your community's needs? What do you want to do together and how should you do this? Who and what do you have available to help you to achieve your goals? When do you want to do this? For what purpose are you doing this together? How you answer these through your words and actions will affect how you and your team or community collaborate with one another to achieve your shared goals.

Together, you will need to make meaningful, long-range and ethical decisions. You'll need to think about how this impacts individuals as well as the community as a whole by seeing the facts and details, exploring possibilities, and balancing the benefits and costs. You will need a process to do this; one model for decision-making that I have been using for myself and my clients for years now involves the following five Ds:

1. **Discover:** what characterises us? What were we like yesterday? What do we look like at our best today? What might we become tomorrow?

2. **Diagnose:** what patterns and trends can we see in the data? What's one thing we are good at that we might become even better at doing? What's one thing we are not so good at doing that we might improve? What's something we are not doing now that we might like to try?

3. **Decide:** what changes do we want to make in who we are becoming? What do we want to leave as is? What differences

do we want to see in ourselves? How might we become stronger in our purpose and practice?

4. **Design:** what's our plan to bring about our desired changes? What steps might we take to make these changes happen? When can we realistically take these steps? What would success look like for us?

5. **Deploy:** what do we need to take the big step forward and up? Is there anything we need to make a start that we don't have in place right now? Who can help us to get going and keep moving? Is there anything else that we haven't yet thought about before we set off?

Once you have worked out what you want to do and connected it to your sense of purpose, writing a plan and making it happen is a great way for you to create clarity for yourself and those around you. Making it happen builds your strength of character and improves your capacity to organise yourself. Refining it as you go builds your adaptability and improves your chance of realising your vision. Even when things don't end up happening as you might want them to, your ongoing process of planning will help you and those in your care to move forward with confidence. It's the work of a lifetime and something worth doing.

Reflection: Planning

Please consider the following questions:

Do I set myself clear targets?

Do I work out the best ways to achieve these aims?

Do I organise my time and focus my energy and resources on achieving my goals?

> Do I check on my progress on an ongoing basis?
>
> Do I use the setting and achievements of goals as a motivator for getting things done in my life?

Project management

Do you know how to turn planning into a specific expertise in making significant projects or initiatives happen? Can you connect your purpose and the purpose of your team or organisation to these projects? Do you manage yourself and other people well in the process?

Project management is how you make choices to build a plan to achieve a specific goal in a timely and resource-effective fashion. Many projects are limited in their time frame; others stretch out in phases that link one goal to another. All projects should, ideally, be linked to a central idea about what you are trying to achieve or a problem you are trying to solve personally, socially or professionally.

There should be, therefore, a reason why you want to make this important thing happen. This reason needs to be part of a story of moving from yesterday to today to tomorrow. The value proposition that sits behind the 'why?' of a project will be critical to unite all of the people involved. After all, if you are going to commit yourself and your resources to doing something, you are better off knowing what you intend and the value that achieving this intention will bring to yourself, to others, to your organisation, and so on.

When you have considered the 'why?', you will need to turn your attention to the 'how?' and the 'what?' and how you will share these with team members and those whom they are serving. This begins with the vision behind the project ('where are we going?'), the vocabulary we will use to describe the strategy ('how will we get there?') and culture ('how will we do things to help us get there?') that you will put into place as a result of the project. Finally, you will need to determine the pace of change that will be used to bring this about – this is what will determine the expectations and standards for performance. It will also influence the values that will be honoured in the process during which this will be brought about. All of this can help to make a project fit for purpose, something of significance that will bring about a meaningful transformation in how you learn, live, lead and work individually or collectively.

Project management skills include organising time, breaking down goals into tasks, allocating roles and resources, supervising and providing feedback, and reporting up, down and sideways in an organisation. There are numerous approaches to this as well as modern project management digital technologies to help link workers to the task and each other.

The key to all of this is structure and flexibility. You must know exactly what must be done, by whom and when. You must also keep an eye on the broad picture so that you can evolve your plan to account for human and other variables as your world and the people in it change.

You'll need to keep open lines of communication and consider how people express themselves while they work together. You'll need to develop standards of behaviour to guarantee you know who you are (the civil character of belonging), how you operate together (the performance character of fulfilling potential) and the values you wish to defend (the moral character of doing of what is good and right). You'll also need to: know how people will be paid (how much and when); maintain the project under budget; know how to make decisions and obtain information to support those decisions; and design processes that bring people together, help them manage their time better and achieve the desired standard.

The knowledge, skills, disposition and habits of project management are among the most important and practical of all the capabilities that you can acquire. As a project manager, you will define the plan and need to stay focused on the tasks at hand. Once a project is underway, you'll need to know how it all fits together, what is likely to come next and why it's all being done. You'll need to hold the team together and grow them in their capacity with the right culture. And, most of all, you will need to do the work and get the job done!

Reflection: Project Management

Please consider the following questions:

Am I able to relate the mission and vision of my organisation to the work of the project at hand and to help those around me understand and be energised by the connection?

Do I bring open-mindedness and the ability to adapt to new information, uncertainty and change to current and future projects?

Do I help my team or group resolve issues that get in the way of progress, tap into everyone's knowledge and ideas, and achieve the desired goals?

Am I good at designing systems and pathways for information gathering, decision-making, implementation and evaluation?

Do I help the team drive towards the most creative and innovative decisions, solutions and results?

Getting it done

Evaluation

Do I use evidence to measure and make decisions about my progress and the success I am achieving? Can I balance this with my intuition? Can I relate this to the bigger story of my life and its journey?

Evaluation and the critical thinking that supports it are such important skills to master. It takes courage to confront the reality that some things you do are not yet good enough to meet the standards required and to achieve your goals. It can be hard to separate this from how you feel about yourself as a person. But if you don't measure how far you have come on your journey and reflect on and make decisions about what you have learned along the way, you can never be sure about what you have really done towards realising your purpose.

It's important for you to know what progress and success look like if you are going to measure how far you have come and how well you are doing. Success criteria can be helpful here. To discover the right success criteria for you and your team, you must first establish what you should expect to see when you achieve your goal. The language you use to do this needs to be clear, measurable and aligned to the language and expectations you and others have for what success means. After all, the measure needs to reflect the goal.

You'll also need to establish and describe the different stages you might reach on the way towards the goal.

As you grow in confidence with how you evaluate and assess yourself, you will become stronger at matching your strengths to a situation (your adaptive expertise) and in how you organise all the elements of who you are to get the job done (your self-efficacy). You will also be more confident in applying your sense of what is right and wrong to the decision-making processes that follow on from measurement. You'll need to work out what processes you will use to make decisions. What evidence will you need? Who will you involve? When will the decision be made? By whom? And why will you adopt these approaches? How and when might you review your decisions, and what would you need to see to change your mind?

As you become more experienced in making judgements about yourself, your work and others – that are supported by evidence, reasonable in their use of your intuition and balanced in terms of their conclusions – you will also become more comfortable with the way you are growing. You will also become more comfortable in yourself. You will come to accept that you are a work in progress who is improving in competency and wellness. This improvement will come about not just because of the specific growth in knowledge, skills, dispositions and habits related to your goals and tasks, but because you are engaged in the process of improvement itself.

You will need to determine the methods you will use to collect information about your process and accomplishments, as well as the people who you will use to provide advice and support. Creating these methods from the beginning gives you the best chance to build rapport with a peer who will give you a frank assessment of your progress. We need to step back from the immediate pressures of getting the work done and look at the whole picture of what is being done and how well it is being done. This requires mental preparation and sometimes physical distance from the site of your work to allow you to form a solid judgement.

In time, you will come to understand that measurement of who you are becoming and what you are doing to make this happen is how you will become more fully yourself. It will help you to understand how you are growing in the civic character of belonging, the performance character of fulfilling your potential and the moral character of doing good and right. In this way, your ongoing process of evaluation and assessment will allow you to bring both values and value to the community around you.

> ### Reflection: Evaluation
>
> Please consider the following questions:
>
> Am I constantly reflecting on my goal-setting process to ensure I am on the right path and using the right tools to get there?
>
> Do I bravely welcome feedback of various sorts in order to improve my performance?
>
> Do I bring balance and reasoning to decisions and actions, assessing whether conclusions and judgements are evidence-informed, soundly determined and appropriate to the circumstances?
>
> Am I good at assessing my knowledge, skills, dispositions and habits, finding out what I need to learn and to be better in achieving my goals?
>
> Do I identify and work on the knowledge, skills, dispositions and habits that I can transfer from other areas of strength that might help me expand my repertoire of competencies and enhance my progress?

Step Forward and Up
Getting it done

Please revisit what you prepared at the end of Chapter 2 to sketch out your sense of purpose and the story of yourself that you want to tell.

It's time now to write some goals for yourself to get this done. Draft three goals that might help you to achieve your social purpose:

- ✓ A **Personal Growth Goal** – one specific goal to improve your capability to achieve your social purpose.
- ✓ A **Team Goal** – one specific goal through which you can achieve your social purpose by helping those closest to you.
- ✓ A **Community Goal** – one specific goal through which you can achieve your social purpose to bring benefit to your broader community.

Your goals will give you the intention and direction you need to plan your journey and (simultaneously) help others.

Next, define what success would look like for each of these goals and when you would like them to happen. The more specific you are about what you would like to achieve, the more likely that you will know what you need to do (and that you will actually do it).

Now you need to think about committing to the action you will take to make these goals real.

Follow these two steps:

1. Check your thinking about your proposed goals. How will you ensure that you manage yourself and others well to achieve your goals? What resources will you need to help you? How will you build and maintain the momentum needed to achieve your goals step by step? Read over your draft goals and success criteria carefully and make any necessary changes.

2. For each of your goals, write a brief summary of how you think the goal might become a reality. Consider using the five W model prompts:

    Why have you chosen to focus on this area, and how does it align with your purpose statement?

    What will you need to do to grow and improve in this area?

    Who might you speak with to gain knowledge and skill in your focus area?

    Planning for the future must be balanced with an objective self-analysis about **where** you currently are; this is where you evaluate what assets you bring, and what limitations are standing in your way.

    When will you dedicate attention to this area for growth and improvement?

This is your plan to **Make a Difference**, your guide to getting it done. It is a bit different to the sort of plan you might write for a specific project, but this is because you can't allow your intentions to become locked in too rigidly. Remember that life happens to us while we are trying to put our intentions into action, so you will need to revisit, review and revise this plan on an ongoing basis.

Conclusion
Let's go!

This **Character Education Series** is all about you – your character, your purpose and how you learn, live, lead and work in the world:

- **A Life of Purpose** – how to identify and claim the fundamental reason why for your journey of exploration, discovery and encounter.
- **The Pathway to Excellence** – how to learn, live, lead and work as you strive to become the best version of yourself.
- **Leading for Tomorrow's World** – how to connect your purpose to leadership which influences, inspires, directs and motivates others to build a shared vision for the future.
- **Make a Difference** – how to create a plan to put your sense of purpose into practice for the sake of people and place and planet.

If you have found what you have learned to be valuable, then please feel free to share your journey and these books with your friends.

Before we finish, there's one final thought I'd like to share with you.

A true story of what makes a difference yesterday, today and tomorrow is a story of what really matters to me, you and us. The story must be real and the lessons revealed in it must show the true nature of our character and how it has been formed. We must tell of the need for reciprocity among people to whom the story matters, for none is complete of themselves and everyone depends on what others bring in their diversity to fill in the gaps. We need to explain the 'why?' and its interdependence with the 'how?' and the 'what?'. We must also be prepared to take offence at what we believe to be untrue and not allow this to perpetuate as a matter of honour.

The values and value proposition that can help you to **Make a Difference** must also be reinforced by a tangible direction that is described within an authentic narrative arc that seeks to describe the passage of this same lifetime.

As leaders, therefore, we hold out to those whom we lead the promise of transformation that must be told through a shared story of aspiration, experience, testing and progress towards a goal, often experiencing the challenge of adversity that bonds people together along the way. What success looks like and the goals associated with this will change as we go.

There needs to be an intentional purposefulness about this, but also a willingness to do things in the moment that allow for free expression, fun and the generation of divergent thinking. They need to be conscious that the pressure of high-stakes accountabilities and confrontations can destroy the way research and development is undertaken. At the same time, it's very useful to know what is expected of us and plan to achieve success.

Over my own lifetime, I've learned that knowing when to adopt a research mindset can be very helpful. Research should always be attentive towards an agreed process but must remain genuinely open about the results of this process. Sometimes a modelled solution or a hypothesis can be useful, but if I impose too many expectations about the end point, I can hamper my capacity to sit at a respectful distance and observe the process as it plays itself out. Alternatively, I can develop a wilful blindness to the outcomes, choosing instead to see what I want, and not what is and must be.

All of this thinking about both the process and product of my work is grounded within an unrelenting commitment to my own progress: taking the big step forward and up. I've got to keep moving forward. Sometimes I try to do this in big leaps (many of which don't work). More often these days, I try to take one step at a time and see how it goes. Thus the 'big step forward and up' to which I have connected you throughout the four books of the **Character Education Series** is most likely a set of much smaller steps joined up by a story.

As we work towards claiming and living out our 'why?' and our 'how?' through our adaptive expertise and self-efficacy, we never really stop. I think that's one of the hallmarks of the process – that constant reinvention and reimagining of what we do, how we do it and of what form the products of our intention and innovation will take. We need to realise our own inner drive by leaving our mark while replicating the expectations of those around us by measuring up.

One of the things I can do to help me leave my mark and measure up is to get up in the morning and just go for it every day. At the same time, I know that I also need to make the time to rest and develop the habit of reflection that will together promote renewal. Because if I don't, who will? And then what reserves of both strength and strategy will I have to help me to make it through the challenge and become the best version of myself that I can be?

A disposition towards action and an unrelenting sense of optimism about what the future brings, coupled with the personal discipline of renewal, can be hard things to hold on to, but they are so very important when our times are filled with uncertainty and our official and unofficial sources of news and information amplify conflict, division and gloom. We need a method for countering this culture of cynicism, a 'how?' to go with the 'why?'

I have come to realise that there are three key features to the method that I typically use to ensure that I keep going forward, which might also help you:

1. **Choose your purpose** – you can't do everything that is asked of you and you can't be all things to all people. If you want to be excellent, you must choose what is important to you and work hard at doing it better over time. You must also care for those with whom you travel on your journey.

2. **Find your crew** – you need to build a team that can become better over time at achieving its purpose. How you choose this team is important. Not everyone will agree with what you think matters most, so you need to identify and build a community of inquiry and practice with those whose vision, values, intention and means align with your own. You need to learn from others, learn with others, do it yourself and share with others. You cannot just construct a bubble to protect yourself from the views of others in the world around you, and you can't simply surround yourself with people who are exactly the same or whose thinking does not challenge and test your own. You need to be deeply invested in the potential of your crew and ensure that the culture of 'how we do things here' allows you to perform and achieve results that both meet expectations and reveal an integrity to your values and how you put them into practice.

3. **Go on an adventure** – you need to experience the world. You need to explore, discover and encounter what is possible. Together with a team of different strengths and ways of seeing

the world, you might do the work of belonging, fulfilling your purpose and doing what is good and right. My most significant colleagues have taught me that it's important to work hard and to develop theories about what works best. They've also helped me to see that it's dangerous to lock these ideas in too early in the process. You need to evolve before we capture, and to plan an approach to learning that research tells you is most likely to work. You need to put this into practice and live through the process in your own context. You also need the gratitude and patience to strive for excellence over time without ever aiming for or achieving perfection. To do this requires you to ascertain the weight of evidence for your views. You need to ask yourself: 'how would you know?'

From this, you might analyse your results and form a hypothesis as to how the process may have led to these results. Then you need to test this hypothesis, iterating the process that sits behind the method based on what you have learned. You need to calibrate this experience to the learning of others who have weighed up what learning looks like across many contexts and adapt your thinking about your earlier hypothesis. Finally, you need to align all of your learning about learning so that you present a narrative about the projected vision, vocabulary, volume and velocity of how you plan to leave your mark on the world, while honouring the expectations of those around you, that you will measure up to shared standards and expectations.

Whatever the plot of your adventure and the sequence of its episodes, I believe that your story of it will be made more powerful if it is:

- **Purpose-driven in form** – do you know your reason 'why?' and can you use this to explain your story and how your purpose arose from it?

- **Rich in experience** – can you explain the things that matter to you and the lessons you have learned? Can you illustrate the pattern of continuity and change in both the grand events and the vicissitudes of life that have propelled your understanding of your purpose?
- **Authentic in ideas and relationships** – do you know how to reveal the truth behind your story? Can you share the pieces of wisdom drawn from connected and relevant anecdotes drawn from experience and relationship that inspire you and inform your reason 'why?'?

Thank you for allowing me to share a bit of my story, my adventure with you. What about you? As a leader, you need to be clear as to why you are doing what you are doing and how you might do it. Have you built a model for your method? And can you tell people your story of how you have done all of this? After all, why should they follow you if they don't know who you are, what you stand for, where you want to take them and how you propose to get there?

For you to tell the story of 'us', you need to begin with the story of 'me'. Every story has a beginning that sets the scene and establishes the premise on which the story is based, a middle where the trajectory is established and lessons learned, and an end which deals with complications and consequences through resolution, and perhaps even a call to action that unites. But you need to be able to tell your own story in a meaningful fashion, freed from the template of traditional narrative – your story needs to be authentic to you, your own trajectory, your own context and how they all intersect with each other. It might not follow a conventional storyline, but it will – most likely – draw on the essence of the human adventure: anticipation, success, struggle, rejection, contemplation, resolution, collaboration, love, learning, growth, progress and the like.

So, tell me a story.

Tell me your story.

Tell me a story of the things that matter.

Tell me a story of the things that matter to you.

Tell me a story of the things that matter to us.

Tell me a story of how you **Make a Difference**.

Life's an adventure.

Let's go!

www.ingramcontent.com/pod-product-compliance
Lightning Source LLC
Chambersburg PA
CBHW070332120526
44590CB00017B/2858